Invasive Species Takeover

AFRICANIZED HONEY- BEES

SCOTT PEARSON

◯ WORLD BOOK

This World Book edition of *Africanized Honeybees* is published by agreement between Black Rabbit Books and World Book, Inc.
© 2017 Black Rabbit Books,
2140 Howard Dr. West,
North Mankato, MN 56003 U.S.A.
World Book, Inc.,
180 North LaSalle St., Suite 900,
Chicago, IL 60601 U.S.A.

All rights reserved. No part of this book may be reproduced in any form without written permission from the publisher.

Design and Production by Michael Sellner
Photo Research by Rhonda Milbrett

Library of Congress Control Number: 2015916878

HC ISBN: 978-0-7166-9697-1   PB ISBN: 978-0-7166-9698-8

Printed in the United States at CG Book Printers,
North Mankato, Minnesota, 56003. PO #1793 4/16

Image Credits

AdobeStock: ivan kmit, 28 (br); Alamy: Gustavo Mazzarollo, 8–9; ars.usda.gov: 22–23 (map); Corbis: Glen Wexler/Masterfile, 1; Klaus Nowottnick, 10; SuperStock, 15; Getty: Andy Roberts, 20; ChinaFotoPress/Stringer, 4–5; Mark Murphy, 12–13 (track); Michael Langford, 16 (top); Otto Hahn, 27; Deb Alperin, 19 (top); Stephen St. John, 6–7; Newscom: Gary Trotter/REX, 28 (tr); Shutterstock: angelshot, 23 (bees); Armita, 16, 26 (map); Brumarina, 26 (top); cartoons, 29; CHAIYA, 28 (bl); claffra, 3, 32; Dancestrokes, Cover; Les Perysty, 16; Loradora, 12–13 (bees), 22–23 (illustrated bees), 31; Merlinul, 18–19 (bees); Photografiero, 24; phugunfire, 28 (tl); Ramona Kaulitzki, 22–23 (comb); tobkatrina, 11; Yuttasak Jannarong, 21

Every effort has been made to contact copyright holders for material reproduced in this book. Any omissions will be rectified in subsequent printings if notice is given to the publisher.

Contents

CHAPTER 1
Attacked by Bees!. . . .4

CHAPTER 2
Out of Africa. 14

CHAPTER 3
The War of
the Bees. 18

CHAPTER 4
Fighting Back. 25

Other Resources. 30

CHAPTER 1

Attacked by

A farmer in Texas drove his tractor over a pile of wood. He heard the wood crunch. Then, he heard buzzing. Suddenly, 40,000 bees were on him. They stung him thousands of times. The farmer couldn't survive.

Strength in Numbers

The attacking bees were Africanized honeybees. These creatures are small but fierce. Most bees attack in small numbers. These bees attack by the thousands. Many people call them "killer bees."

THE KILLER BEE UP CLOSE

HEAD

THORAX

ANTENNA

Invasive Species

Killer bees were not supposed to be in Texas. Several years ago, some of the bees left Brazil. They quickly spread to new places. They hurt animals and plants that already lived there. Killer bees are an **invasive species**.

CHAPTER 2

Out of

Long ago, no honeybees lived in North or South America. In 1622, beekeepers brought European bees to North America. Some bees then traveled to South America. But it was too hot for them there.

In 1956, a scientist in Brazil had an idea. African bees like warm weather. But they are mean. He decided to **breed** African and European bees together.

First Sightings of Killer Bees in the United States

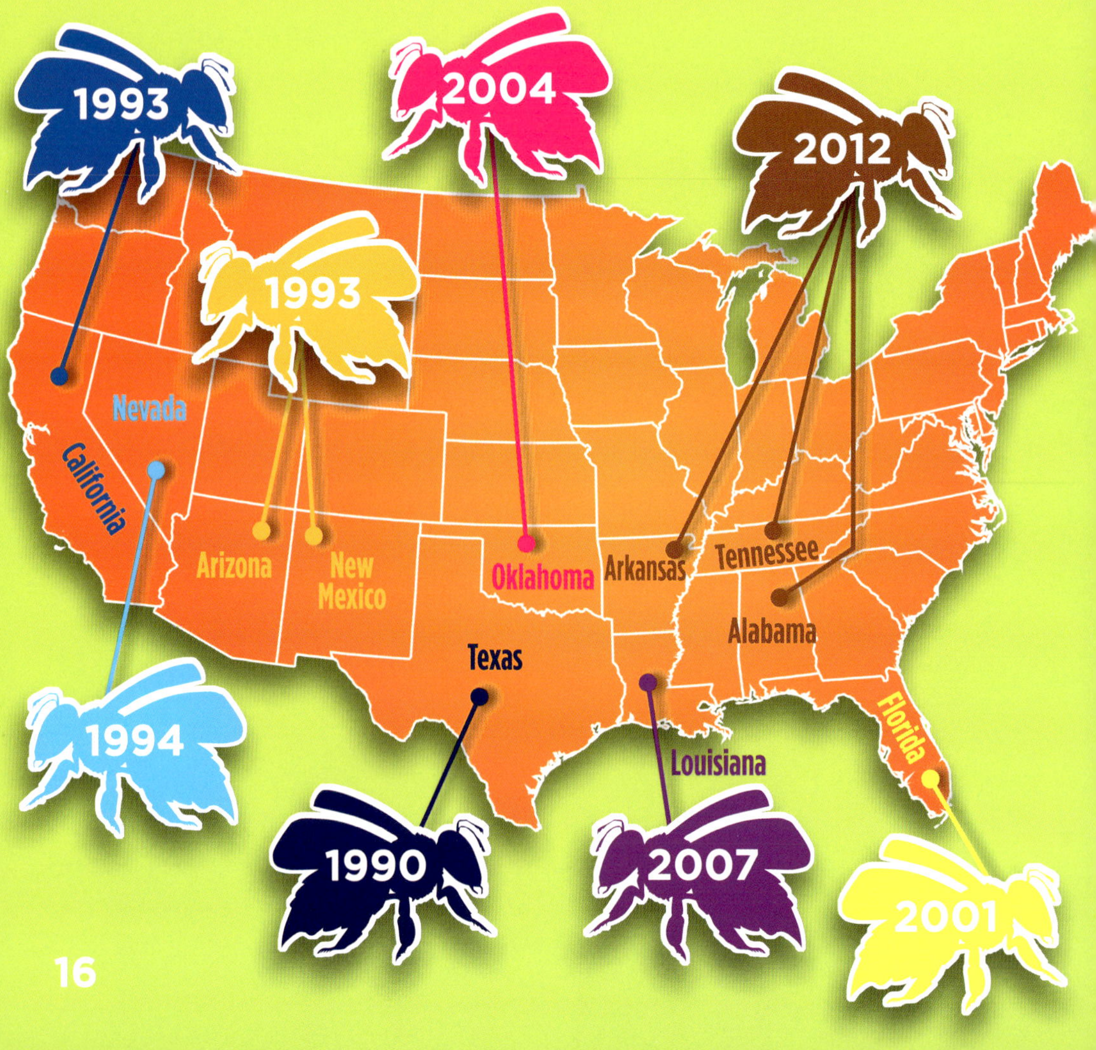

Not What He Planned

The scientist thought the new bees would be calm. He also hoped they would make honey in tropical weather. But the new bees were not calm. The "Africanized" bees were fierce.

In 1957, the bees escaped from the lab. They **swarmed** into Central America and Mexico. Later, they reached the United States.

CHAPTER 3

The War of the

Killer bees have killed at least 1,000 people. Many more people have survived attacks. Attacks increase as the bees move into cities.

Killer bees sting two Arizona women hundreds of times.
2010

2011
Bees kill a Texas couple. Their son is injured.

Bees attack a Florida man and his dog. Firefighters helping them are stung too. The people survive but the dog dies.

2013

2012

A California woman is stung more than 100 times. Her gardener is stung about 80 times.

2014

At least 800,000 bees attack people in Arizona. One person dies and four more are injured.

Food Fight

Killer bees cause problems for other bees too. Bees eat **nectar** and **pollen**. Killer bees compete with other bees for this food. With less food to go around, bees make less honey.

Get Off My Lawn!

Killer bees are very protective of their nests. A loud noise 50 feet (15 m) away can bring a cloud of angry, stinging bees.

Queen of the Hive

Killer bees take over other beehives. African **worker** bees land on a hive. They wait until they are allowed in. Then, they kill the European **queen** and replace it with their own.

The Spread of Killer Bees

- 1990-2000
- 2001
- 2002
- 2003
- 2004
- 2005
- 2006
- 2007
- 2008
- 2009
- 2010
- 2011

CHAPTER 4

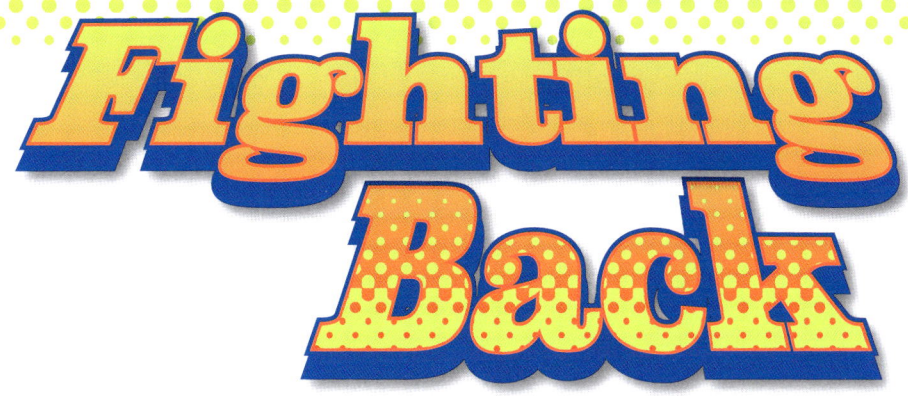

People are trying to slow the spread of killer bees. Beekeepers often put new European queens in their hives. The change can keep African queens from taking over.

Some scientists say releasing more European **drones** into the wild could help. Then European queens are less likely to breed with killer bees. Fewer killer bees would be born.

Making Peace with Killer Bees

Killer bees are more dangerous than other honeybees. But they do some good. Like other honeybees, killer bees **pollinate** plants. So say thanks, but don't get too close.

Don't Cross the Line

Killer bees can't survive in cold climates.

34 degrees north latitude

KILLER BEES BY THE NUMBERS

1
NUMBER OF TIMES A KILLER BEE CAN STING BEFORE IT DIES

960
NUMBER OF STINGS AN AVERAGE 12-YEAR-OLD COULD SURVIVE

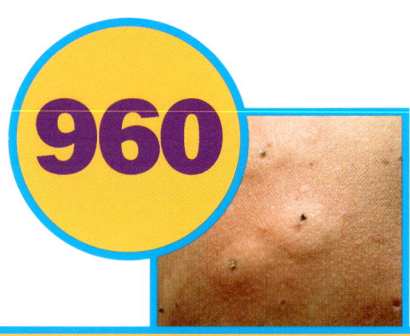

200 MILES
(322 kilometers)
DISTANCE KILLER BEES CAN SPREAD IN A YEAR

100 FEET
(30 m)
SAFE DISTANCE AWAY FROM A KILLER BEE HIVE

5 TO 10 WEEKS
LENGTH OF A DRONE'S LIFE

Think about It...

1. Honeybees die after they sting. Use other sources to find out why stinging kills the bees.

2. A scientist bred two kinds of bees and created killer bees. Should scientists be allowed to cross animals? Explain why or why not.

3. Africanized honeybee attacks increase when the bees reach big cities. Why does that happen?

GLOSSARY

breed (BREED)—to bring together to produce babies

drone (DRONE)—a male bee that has no stinger and doesn't gather food

invasive species (in-VAY-siv SPEE-seez)—animals or plants that spread through an area where they are not native, often causing problems for native plants and animals

nectar (NEK-tuhr)—a sweet liquid given off by plants and flowers

pollen (PAH-len)—powdery, yellow grains on flowering plants

pollinate (PAH-luh-nayt)—to move pollen from one plant to another; this action allows plants to grow new seeds.

queen (KWEEN)—a female bee that lays all the eggs in a hive

swarm (SWARM)—to move together in a crowd

worker (WURK-ur)—a female bee that has a stinger and gathers nectar and pollen

LEARN MORE

LEARN MORE

Machajewski, Sarah. *Killer Bees.* Things that Sting! New York: Gareth Stevens Publishing, 2016.

Owings, Lisa. *Killer Bees.* Nature's Deadliest. Minneapolis: Bellwether Media, Inc., 2013.

Riggs, Kate. *Bee.* Grow with Me. Mankato, MN: Creative Paperbacks, 2015.

WEBSITES

Encyclopedia Smithsonian: Killer Bees
www.si.edu/encyclopedia_si/nmnh/buginfo/killbee.htm

Invasive Species: Animals– Africanized Honeybee
www.invasivespeciesinfo.gov/animals/afrhonbee.shtml

Killer Bees!
www.youtube.com/watch?v=d-7kKqgPEGs

INDEX

B

body parts, 8–9

C

creation of Africanized honeybees, 14, 17

D

deaths, 4, 18–19

F

food, 21

I

introduction to nonnative areas, 11, 16–17, 22–23

L

life span, 28

N

nests, 21, 22, 25, 28

S

stopping spread, 25